This Girl, Your Disciple

poems by

Susan L. Leary

Finishing Line Press
Georgetown, Kentucky

Susan L. Leary

This Girl, Your Disciple

To the vision of my mother

"What was torn away is speaking."

—Forrest Gander
"To Eurydice"

ACKNOWLEDGMENTS

I am most thankful to the University of Miami College of Arts and Sciences for granting me a Summer Research Award, which provided the time, knowledge, and strength to work on these poems.

I am equally indebted to the venues in which some of these poems first appeared, at times in earlier versions:

Arcturus (Chicago Review of Books): "Weather Events: Fog"
After the Pause: "The Gazelle"
Clear Poetry: "Before She Died" & "The Visitors"
Cold Creek Review: "Stratfield Road, February 1961"
Crack the Spine: "This Girl, Your Disciple"
Dying Dahlia Review: "Two Truths"
Gyroscope Review: "First Appointment (circa 1958)"
Into the Void: "The Rose Mallow"
Lady Blue Literary Arts Journal: "He Was a Good Man"
Not One of Us: "Fatherless Daughter Syndrome"
Steel Toe Review: "Thinking Clearly"
Sweet Tree Review: "How I Am Born"
The Christian Century: "Eighth Day"

I am grateful to Barbara Ashcroft, for gathering everyone and for loving unconditionally; to Patricia Brennan, for her imagery and imagination; to Helen Stonkas, for enduring; and to everyone else, for sharing what they could remember.

Thank you to Philip Elliott, Maureen Seaton, and Jaswinder Bolina, for their kind words; to Bob T., for the book, *325th Medical Battalion: Medics of the Century*; to DP, for the journal, in which many of these poems were first penned; and to Bennett, for making me believe I could do this.

Thank you also to my parents, especially my mom, who knows these poems better than I do, and to my husband, Sean, without whom, not much would be possible.

Publisher: Leah Maines
Editor: Christen Kincaid
Cover Art: Susan L. Leary
Author Photo: Sean M. Kilpatrick
Cover Design: Elizabeth Maines McCleavy

Printed in the USA on acid-free paper.
Order online: www.finishinglinepress.com
            also available on amazon.com

Author inquiries and mail orders:
Finishing Line Press
P. O. Box 1626
Georgetown, Kentucky 40324
U. S. A.

Table of Contents

The Rose Mallow

Daybreak   and even at the start   —from itself,
it flees: a flowering hibiscus,

beet-pink and heady with self-announcement.
Look there.
     Every blood-orange center born
         of a bowstring. The petals taut
     and meticulous in their pulling
back ... The whole of it desirous of the mouthfeel

of rain. The whole of what was wanting to be said:

disregarded. Might the leaves,
edged with
     teeth, teach relaxation, teach the way out
       of such imprecise attention?

How the emeraldness gathers and spreads —
     crawls through atmosphere,

delivers afternoon   and with it,
     a flower akin to coral in a deep sea.
       Sun and water slackening in the fullness.

Though by evening, look again:
an underside
     the color of flesh. The powdery wings of a thousand
     moths

     falling
     asleep at the stalk. The flower shriveling so as
       to feel for itself,

         conscious, in the last breath,
         of something missed.

As if to say,
      there is the muddied earth,

      there is the dead
      rain,

but what of my body
will I remember?

Weather Events: Fog

The rain stopped after raining for weeks
and suddenly the world resembled your bones.
This was midnight. Before the woman
asleep upstairs is a widow. The gutters emptied
of their secrets. It doesn't take long
for you to grow complacent in your suffering.
At the kitchen table, the chill of February
ever-awake in your hands. Outside, a thick fog
moves in and obliterates the dampened spines
of trees. The ground covered in branches
that have snapped their necks. The coroner says
4-6 minutes. But how long, I want to ask,
did you know you were close to dying?
So long, perhaps, that as you finally rise
you forget every light in the house will be left
on for her. A dream of your daughters' sunlit
dresses hanging to dry. The line perfectly
knotted. In several hours, men will stumble
across the muddied lawn, carrying your body,
stiff and bloated, from the cellar. Cold air heavy
with the breath of neighbors who cannot help
but talk. The next day it rains. The sky still
bruised from the scrape of your chair. Your swift
fingers. Though in whose bones, I want to ask,
will this woman continue to wake?

First Appointment (circa 1958)

You would be my age. Mid-thirties. Married almost
ten years. Bodies tremulous in your separate chairs.

The room is made of mahogany. The man you've
sought a kind of god, ashing a cigarette into the desk.

Books are everywhere, opened like prayers. Which,
you wonder, contains the parable of your husband?

The day you wed, you didn't know what it would be like:
being with a man. But for a brief moment, the psychiatrist

is a priest, begging of you promises. He is proud to teach
you how to tell yourself what happened. How to look

at your husband with a gentle fondness. By the third
cigarette, you have learned words like *neurotic*. Though

how wretched must I be to assume a great distance between
you? To question if there were love before, even while,

the man you agree to a life with disappears within himself
from the Reserpine? Prefers to you his mother. How I

ache for you to have returned home, pressed your sodden
body to his. Balled your fists into his chest and screamed

you loved him. Perhaps you did. The spring rain
unrelenting: my mother born January of the next year.

The Gazelle

Like the mind unable to rid itself of an idea, so the gazelle,
satisfied by drink, lingers
by the river's edge,
attuned to the uncurling of his spindly legs
and the splendor of his hoofs
alight on the dried mud. He is certain,
today,
that the crocodile will let him live, so unfazed
the yellow-eyed beast has been
by the usual tip-toe
or ear-twitch,
indolent, full-bellied, and self-important
he sleeps,
some yards away, at the center of the near-evaporated water.
The gazelle will not learn
to grant the crocodile respect
nor to see any threat
separate from the creation
of his own tale,
even as all that surrounds him is wary. Sharp
blades of grass
startle each other
into consciousness. The water, panicked
by its own symmetry,
closes in on itself
faster than it desires. Wearied and impatient,
a many-limbed
tree is humbled by the throat-cries
of birds who suffer within the tangled respite. Back home from war,
what are you to be vigilant of?
The footfall of soldiers
carrying dead bodies back to your camp?
The force of your wounded
hands in wounds?

Only more wounds,
bodies writhing from the pain of self-knowledge.
Like the gazelle, bewildered
by his own thirst, you will stand
hoof-high
on a bench in the basement
and kick it out from under you, heaving
with self-convincing
unambivalence, so that you might
let the crocodile eat you, so paralyzed you are waiting at the bank
by your own awareness of the possibility.

The Visitors

It would have been nice had someone talked about it
when the world declared its second war.
For all the women, the headline might have read:
Truman will drop an atomic bomb so that more men
may drop in on doorsteps.
And they will drop in:
in the morning, in the evening, in the afternoon,
tomorrow and for decades—
to visit the grieving wives and mothers
who have words for God but no words for all the suicides
by strangulation,
the exhaust pipes shimmied through windows,
nor the pills, scattered like bullets, on nightstands.
It will be the right thing,
the Nazis might have said, for men to stop by for a warm meal
made by the hands of a self-composing woman
who will take their coats and hats and hang them
properly in the closet,
before showing them where to go.
In the kitchen, she will get out the good china
and the good glasses
for a brandy, or a coffee, or a whiskey sour.
So that it's not much unlike how it was before:
because sitting in a distant room,
in the good chair, is one more man—looking around,
waiting for his peas and carrots and slice of pork
chop—who won't ever talk about it.

Parallels

Beginning with,   winter: & a body of water
that   refuses
        to leave. From the awnings,   icicles enduring
a slow death—   mercury clotting like a vein.

Under no circumstance is precision enough to make a thing
        manageable,   even less so: rare.

Not the swatting of a fly,
          nor frantic wind chased into the glass by God.

Months later   & at the door,   a swallow lumbering
       in circles,
          —the early dieback of lilacs overtaken
by blight: the yard still fragrant of a violence.

How any of this is … *for the best?*   Inside, all the hinges
have   rusted—   thus,   the escaping   smell

      of soured milk / bad meat.   Of damp laundry
musting in the cellar.

At certain angles, it can be that looking too long at a thing,
       rather, not long enough,   as with a hard rain

or   measured   sunrise: the way something else
is always   far better at superintending   its grief,

      despite offerings of expediency everywhere.

How simple to snap the fall's   chrysanthemums
at their skulls / break   clean the wings from the hidden

      spine of a bird—:   hurry the process.

In another life, we might see ourselves   *through*— forfeit
     the stubbornness of our very

hands,   allow needle
        to slip through thread,   or vice versa.

Did you know?   A body holds grief in the space between
         want & ruin   *—a phantom limb,*

& outside, it is snowing.
    Everything returns as water.

He Was a Good Man

The poem I want to write is the one I cannot.
There is no metaphor in *He was a good man.*
Truth cannot unconstitute itself.
The pony cannot turn her blonde mane.
He was a good man, she is sure.
Flowers sprout from the dirt into endless patterns of stars.
Everywhere there are steeples of lupine,
white daisies,
and purple heads of aster.
Against the light, their shadows fall on misshapen rocks
built like desks into the ground.
There is no euphemism in their shapes—no trick
or condescension.
Beyond the hill, lamps of sunshine pass through openings in leaves
that have overlapped to make space for their own silhouettes.
This is the divinity of perspective,
and it is here, that the pony grazes unalone and sincere.
Prophetic in her aging,
she will await a time that she may lie down to die, when wildflowers,
unbetrayed by their nature, bend against
her burrowing weight. Uncoaxed, she will think:
The flowers are good to me.
They have loved me more than life.
Legs ready to root the earth with hoofs of blotted ink.
What is the meaning in this final day?
He was a good man, the poem speaks.

Fatherless Daughter Syndrome

for Karen

When I was ten, you told me a story of animal
bones buried among the Black-eyed
Susans of your front yard. How in an afternoon
you pulled to the side of the road and held a dead
thing in your hands. Traced the enormity
of its wounds. I think you wanted to love your father
like that. Be able to love your father like that.
Make him a grave to calm your trembling.
Spawn flowers from a violent earth.
But a woman who was once your mother is still
at a kitchen sink. Roots tangled in her mouth.
Everything scrubbed clean.
She does not know she succeeds at creating
complexities about who you believe
yourself to be. Even at eight, you want for dirt
beneath your fingernails. Think you can grow
a ghost in your lungs. Cough up a voice
for this man to speak to you from. But as you press
your ear to the bloodied ground, the world
is silent. Your father a dream of rabbit
bones. The sunken ribcage an empty garden.

Comprehension

Or perhaps empathy, I'm not sure which,
is a lot like the difficulty in describing to someone
a person's voice,
when that someone hasn't heard that person talk before,
& then too much is believed to be held
by that sound, so difficult
I'm not sure it can even be approximated: in fact, trying
might make it worse,
might make it so
that person becomes less accessible than before,
even as someone, very badly,
wants to receive that person's words, because those words,
real & at their best,
still could not articulate what is really sought for,
& so then, the better.

On Brokenness

Until turning
　　　from where she stood

at the stove, and dropping
to her knees,

　　　she flung open the cellar
　　　door,

and pleaded with me
　　　to　*end　this*—

　　　Do it!　Please!

The words themselves
aggressive,
　　　quick,

devastated by the shame
of their necessity,

　　　the ladle clanging
　　　　　on the linoleum.

And when she made it,
finally,
　　　to me,
　　　　　a scalded animal

slumped
within its frame,

the smell of carrot
　　　and onion

seeped into the skin,

I didn't have to tell her
the body develops

an unkindness—
that it must sharpen

its edges
to call its own
bluff,

as, into my stomach,
her mouth now goaded

what it knew
was coming,

believing that the only way
to withstand it ...

and with her head
in my hands,

I never felt sadder,

more broken

in my life.

Etymology of a Missing Suicide Note,
Found Forty-Eight Years Later

Obituary (n.)—: first use, 1706,
as in "a register of deaths" | meaning, a list of *sought-after* persons
    by God. Thus, second use (also n.)—: anything

that resembles a disappearance,
specifically: a troubling one | as in, removed from a filing
    cabinet or drawer | as in, a body
            of text floated
            down the river |
    often: pertaining to the intentions of a woman.

However, more like
        third use (adj.)—: of, or relating to, the opposite
of buried | as in, marked by the thick scent of upturned
    blossoms
        conspiring in the dirt | as in, evocative of *the exposed*
roots,
    usually: as a result
        of faulty defenses | From the Latin *obitus*, also:
"a departure,"
    literally: "pertaining to death," such as, "dead several hours"
        | or "found in the basement" |

    | or "surviving" | as in, a small boy or grown man
        bent above the earth,
      combing the hardened soil for flowers.
Hence, fourth use (v.)—: *to dig*, primarily: to dig by making oneself
    a grave | to, subsequently,
        leave a house
          in ruins | to leave evidence …
Of the truth, thus—: the difference between telling a lie
    & being in denial, particularly as it relates to the person
      or persons
        on the receiving end.

In other words, fifth use (also v.)—: to exist in a rarefied state |
          to confront, continuously, any document
     deemed insufficient |
               for example, "a brief biological sketch,
                    especially in a newspaper" |
as with the following:
          In 1961, Charles W. _____ was given "a verdict of
          suicidal strangulation by hanging."

Given these circumstances,
          also: frequently used as an abbreviation—: as in, *obit*,
                    principally: shorthand for PTSD | as in (*obsolete*),
a euphemism
          or sugarcoat for stress in an interior environment |
          not often: paired with the expressions, "died unexpectedly"
               or "died peacefully at home."

Though, in the plural, *obituaries*—: suggesting movement |
          for example: an insistent expanse of
                    terrain | especially: an insistent expanse of terrain
on the internet |
          as in, an *active* search | as in, a collection of
                    orphaned flowers
                    floating
                         downstream.
In this same vein, from medieval Latin,   ✦
          a derivative of *obire*—: "to go forth, go to meet,"
                    such as: in an encounter |
          typically: an encounter with
                    the ghost of a future
                         loved one or the ghost of
                              a future self.

Yet mostly as in, *just added*: sixth use (adj.), 2009—:   meaning,
         nothing accidental,
                  with the exception of: *reading this* | as in, inevitable
         | as in, having the potential to be photocopied
                           or inked on skin:

                  to be kept, vigorously, alive.

For further learning, *see also*: destiny | miracle | fate |
See, especially, each morning—:   the single flower,
                           with its quivering lilt,
                                    that comes back begging for dawn.

Eighth Day

Hanging behind the cellar stairs: finally,
he rested.
But on the eighth day, God thought better of it
and made possible the tenderest of thefts:
that of milk-white bones plumbed by the heavens
and dug up for the grief-stricken to see.
For all, God said: *Let there be light*
where there is dark.
Let there be truth in an empty sea—but once,
answers in their absence.
And so, the angels were given the most vigilant of tasks:
to part, on only a moonless night, the grass-covered
dirt of graves.
(For how else in this circumstance can love be shown
but with a desire for morbid things?)
And by taking in the rotting skin—and eyes that escape
their sockets like spools
of unwinding thread: *Let each prepare to emerge*
from the earth, carrying as firewood—skeletons:
to hasten speech.
So that muddied and draped in lilies, with still-blind eyes
amok in plea—*Look*, God will say:
Did you not know
the stars are your grandfather's bones
strung as letters in the sky?

Thinking Clearly

The priest,
he assures us he is in heaven,
that he made it through the gates because he was not in his right mind,
because he was not thinking clearly.
Thank God for his suffering.
But his Son,
did he not willingly carry the cross?
Did he not choose to die
for our sins?
This story,
it is one of sacrifice, empathy, validation,
not a technicality of reason.
So I want to say:
Was Jesus
thinking clearly?
Was Jesus
in his right mind?
Might it be that we have gotten it wrong?
Why yes, and on the third day,
he climbed out from under his self-made tomb
and rose again.

Gratitude

for M.K.

People are dying out:
        and you are the last one left—: you,

who we will learn,
        have tended to his stone.

        So we must go to you.

Because something made you go back
to that cemetery,

        my mom says,

saying it each time as if she is crying out
and cannot figure out why.

Because it is unbelievable,
        when seventeen—:   you,

thinking it to be about his back,
        would come & wheel the lawnmower

        out from the garage
            to cut the grass,

and eat, later, a tuna sandwich
he made you
        before taking the bus home.

So it is more peaceful: all these years
through that field,

where, with a screwdriver,
    you will dig along the side of his stone

    to keep the grass
        from growing on it.

Good, then: we have come
to hear it.

Because knowing, all this time,
    there has been not knowing,

makes it profound, and resembles
something of closure.

But is more like gratitude,

    and so necessary that is
    before you go.

Two Truths

My aunts think my Nana's favorite
color was pink.
They wore it, both of them,
the day of her funeral.
My mom thinks her favorite
color was blue.
It matched her eyes.
Even my Nana said she could
really wear it,
& that for a woman,
especially at the time, to prefer blue
was imaginative.
When my mom & I went back
to the house seven years
after it had sold,
& we saw it undressed
of its original wallpaper
with the bright, sky-drawn patterns
of roosters & teapots,
there were traces
of bubble-gum in every room,
like liquid medicine.
But everyone is too young
to recall this.
Before he hung himself
in the basement, my grandfather
built that house,
& he would have painted it for her.
Did she like pink? we are asked.
No, we say,
shaking our heads: *blue*.

I. Helen

after Lyrae Van Clief-Stefanon

The truth:
There are no ships—:

> My husband is dead
> by his own hands,

>> & I am thought a cruel
>> woman.

On the schoolyard,
> one question prevails with
> a wounding

innocence—:

> *Did your mother kill
> your father?*

The truth:
There are no wars, only
myths—:

> I am but guilty of loving
> a man,

>> & women mistake me
>> for a beautiful
>> woman,

a prized horse led into town
to be coaxed

> of her secrets.

Tell me—:   What is it
        that you envy
             or fear?

The truth:
Look at me—:   I am deprived even of
            my own ghost

    & there is no one
    daring to cross

          this sea …

II. Paris

after Lyrae Van Clief-Stefanon

I am convinced our ghosts
were birthed
    before us,

& Zeus the bearer
of storms,

    that we might fall
    to earth
        with the rain ...

The truth:
Returning from war, I am
    no prince,

but from the upper
floor of the shared
    decker,

    I spend afternoons
    waiting for you to appear

    on the horizon,

carrying packaged meat
& bags of fruit
    for your mother.

Your every move
    is graceful—:   to make up

    for the ways
    in which I am not.

Birds drink,
slowly,
your marrow—: fly
        from your chest,

& when you agree,
at last, to a date,

        I choose my words
        carefully.

How to tell you without
        sounding ungrateful?

There is no golden
apple,
        no Aphrodite,

                that you, I discover
                on my own,

& in some distant future,
        upon discovering

        my ill-mannered
        body,

you will see
I do not mean to ruin us.

The truth:
Helen—: Whenever I looked upon
your face,

I felt conspicuously
      alive,

           & from a dew-swept
           arc in the ether,

           I see you now:

                I am breathing.

How I Am Born

Again, it happened last night,
that dream, where, we are hanging exactly where it occurred,
though upside-down, each other
watching,
& it's there: the shelf,
four steps to the right of the bottom of the stair,
as a girl I counted,
& then to ten, as by nine,
sometimes eight, I would have reentered the world
carrying a can of soup or jar
of meat sauce,
my back kept turned to what I know now to be your face,
but really
your hands moving: determining the shape of my nose,
my eyes,
lips,
then my scalp,
tipped, what it feels like,
toward you,
as you saw me before I ever was, in the moment just after: but really
just before that,
though it's already done, & so eclipses itself …
so brief—
this is how I am born,
as you imagine me into what will make me specifically
myself
when you think, *Ah, what have I done?*

Notes on Genetics

"As if a single scream / gave birth // to whole families / of traits // such as 'flavor,' 'color,' / 'spin' // and this tendency to cling."
—Rae Armantrout, "Close"

But of you, all traces have been torn from the house,
& so I cannot inherit your belongings.

No wonder it has come to this:

Morning again & still I spend nights solving for X.
This means I must solve for absence or vacancy or erasure.

I take copious notes & often it is determined I am a very sad girl.
Othertimes, I find I am an altogether

> *indeterminate* function. All of which suggests

the blade is dull. That despite force, it is highly unlikely a person
should be evenly divided.

& so lately, I have become a slow-moving glacier. I am all
calving & write poems in the margins of too many wrong places.

Did you hear the oldest underground pocket of water is estimated
to be 2.6 billion years old?

This means it is *before*-life: a time capsule of an inherited earth.
Though I am weary of digging.

> In Calculus, there is something called a limit.

Of a function, it is the best prediction of a point yet to be observed.
I know because I am good with numbers,

as are you, your Calculus notebooks lining the basement shelves
with the smell of decipherable history.

That they are here suggests at some point they were assumed harmless,
uninstructional. Though I am not so sure.

It's an unsophisticated math,
but the earth's surface is three-quarters water,

       & if my body were the earth, you would be what remains.

Vis-à-vis

"A baby is born with 20/400 vision and is able to see clearly only 8-12 inches in front of her."
—American Academy of Pediatrics

While of course this has changed,
some facts are simply too beautiful to forgo.

So that in putting you in the car
under the fir trees on the side of the house,

I keep my face close to your jocund little body,
thinking you the most uncomplicated thing.

Behind me, the sun is up, and your mother cleans
the autumn air with the newly-hung wash.

The grass blades are as long and coarse as the strings
of an instrument, and your hair is butter-white.

We have been told to make a day for ourselves,
and I reason maybe we will go for ice cream.

Except that we don't, and instead, we stay there
for hours. Just like that. Nose to almost nose,

the glint of my pen rushing stars into the blue
of your eyes. Long enough so that in an evening

when this day should return to you in your sleep,
you will know I am your father.

That in the grander scheme, all I wished
for you was love.

Before She Died

It's grown more difficult to place her in my mind
        in her own house,
where she sits—with knowledge,
        or maybe not that
but thought itself,
        and how it gets away and *just is,*
and might, in fact, be more like inhabiting a mood
        or an act of becoming.
So then, the rocker,
        the one at the foot of her bed,
or maybe she is in the kitchen,
        at the table, where the air conditioner sticks out
from the window too near her head,
        or the lawn chair, yes—a few feet out from the garage,
the kind that is actually a chair and not low
        to the ground,
because she has just pruned the bushes
        and cleaned out the poison ivy,
but no—she is too old for that.
        So I'm thinking she is tucked into the couch,
exactly where the arm meets the back,
        feet propped,
slippers strewn beside the stool,
        half-overturned so you can't fully see the satin,
but you know it's there,
        the ones, that, in Filene's we'd find them,
hanging,
        in maybe August or September
but for Christmas,
        and pick from the back the one in the best box.
And how she looks sitting,
        that I know:

the image, to describe it—it's so severe, almost
        brutal—the first jut
of the knuckles,
        and then the roll of her fist,
like a track within the gear, pushed hard
        though it goes along its path,
and into the side of her face,
        how unforgiving the knuckles are,
right away and after a while, against the cheek bone,
        such a dull ache,
and how she keeps it there
        so aware of her gums in her mouth,
not moving,
        and how it's somewhat self-persuaded,
but also a little innate, so that a few days before it happens,
        with:
Karyl, You don't know how hard my life has been—
        That, just that,
is what she means,
        and just that,
                is saying something.

Stratfield Road, February 1961

'Charlie?' she called
every other step. The baby,
half-asleep in her arms,
until she turned
to head back up the basement stairs:
the night, the spilled
pot of soup,
literally, behind her.
But my Nana had fifty years
to replay the image
of her husband
suspended from the rafters
with the white cord
he bought her the day before
to hang clothes
in the backyard—
while my mother, only two,
cried just once over
her dead father.

The Ruth Clay

Behold in the white light of noon,
a gathering of pink-tinted peonies flowering at the desk,

each colossal head rounding itself,
sweetly, into the bomb-shape of an heirloom.

The blooms as beautiful as expected, effusive of cold
cream & the fresh scent of rose oil.

Our bodies, on the other hand, resist such imagery.
They are not so beautiful.

Even in the glass, the lemon-green stalks are given chance
to bare an intricate architecture, a crisp sheen.

Though we are more misguided, more housefly
landed on the sill in perpetual want of a vaster hour.

Why is it spring should be the only season to hunger
after its history & we do not know what it means

to be generous? After lunch, the furthermost petals
will begin their softening back,

the remaining tufts of bloom feathering out
into a single orb, blithesome & occupied with living.

What we would give to be this immense
& unrefraining?

> To welcome the body with the mildness we do
> a single flourish,

> trusting it to camber into the entirety of our hands,
> saying:

Touch me.
I ask nothing of you in return.

This Girl, Your Disciple

As Joseph of Arimethea,
of whom must I beg permission to build this tomb
for your disappearing? To throw seed
among the crags of rock in hope of mistake
of the briefest flower?
What will Pilate—or anyone—care if I endure
the prick of steel and thorns upon my fingers:
if with grace, it is I to cut
the fibrous cord: loosen the self-hammered
nails: look upon the open mouth that cannot bear
its own breath?
If mild and softhearted, I will lick not dust from my lips,
but a miracle from yours:
ready they might be for wine
or supper or a story—after your body is washed
in aloe and myrrh,
the limbs made gentle in sweet-smelling cloth.
Might it be that you come dressed
for explanation?
That I find resplendent the imprint of your face:
truthful, holy, never treasonous?
Might we be moved—
as was Joseph—with the first appearance of the sun
to speak our own implication?
I cannot know.
But tilled among the fetal sobs and woolly screams
for mercy—(in the cellar: *Get him down!*
Don't touch him!
they say)—a sinew of lung, heart, and spine:
my body a tomb that gardens
your suffering. *Yours, Grandfather:*
forever into blood-red roses.

CPSIA information can be obtained
at www.ICGtesting.com
Printed in the USA
JSHW010402030919
1318JS00001B/5